Science experiments and amusements for children

73 easy experiments (no special equipment needed) illustrate important scientific principles

formerly titled "Science Games for Children"

by CHARLES VIVIAN

Photographs by S.A.R. Watts

DOVER PUBLICATIONS, INC., NEW YORK

CONTENTS

This Dover edition, first published in 1967, is an unabridged and unaltered republication of the work originally published by Sterling Publishing Company, Inc., in 1963 under the title *Science Games for Children*.

This work is reprinted by special arrangement with The Printed Arts Company, Inc., and is for sale in the United States of America, its dependencies and the Philippine Islands only.

Standard Book Number: 486-21856-2
Library of Congress Catalog Card Number: 67-28142
Manufactured in the United States of America
Dover Publications, Inc., 180 Varick Street, New York, N.Y. 10014

Making an Air-Screw

You will need: Stiff drawing paper or thin card, ruler, pencil, scissors, compass, cork, needle.

Warm air always rises. With a constant source of heat, we can use a current of warm air to turn a miniature turbine or "air-screw."

Take the drawing paper or card, set the compass to 2 inches and draw a circle on it. Reset the compass to half an inch and draw a smaller circle inside the larger.

Carefully cut around the larger circle and then rule 16 or 18 lines across the paper disc, in the manner shown in the diagram.

Cut along these radiating lines but stop each cut at the edge of the inner circle.

To create the turbine-wheel you must give each blade a slight twist, each in the same direction. When the blades have been carefully set in this fashion, insert the blunt end of a needle into the end of a cork and balance the "air-screw" on the point of the needle.

Make sure that the little turbine turns easily on its needle mounting. Now place the completed instrument above a source of heat, such as a radiator or even a lighted lamp. As the warm air rises, it will come in contact with the blades of the air-screw and set the wheel spinning. The greater the heat the faster the wheel will spin.

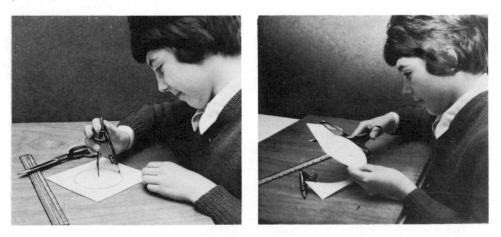

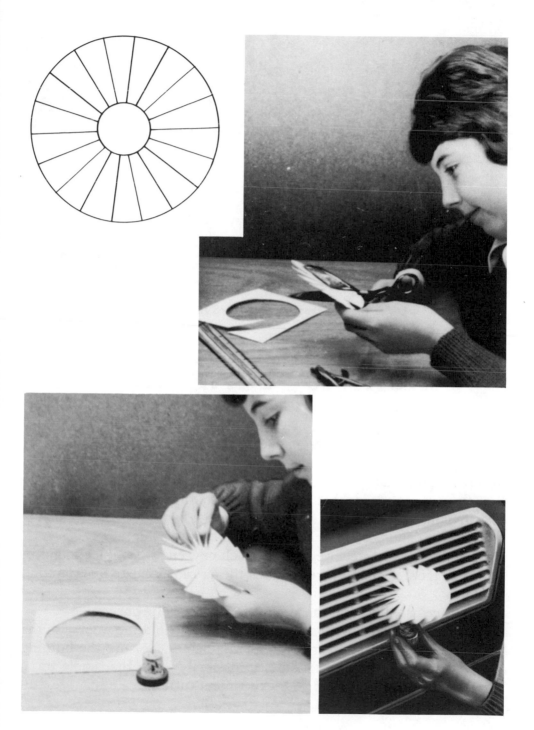

5

Lower the steel wool gently toward the candle flame

How to Burn Steel

You will need: Candle, tongs or pliers, steel wool.

Oxygen is necessary if we wish to burn anything. There are many ways of proving this. One of the simplest is shown here.

You may not realize that steel can burn, although this is done every day in industry with the aid of an extremely hot flame obtained by mixing pure oxygen and acetylene. We will use a candle flame!

In order to burn steel we need as much oxygen as possible around it. We need the steel in fine shreds so that the air can circulate freely around them.

The steel wool used in the kitchen is ideal for our purpose.

Take a tuft of steel wool and fluff it out. Now hold the wool with the tongs or pliers and lower it to the candle flame. (Be sure the burning embers will fall onto a metal surface, preferably into the candle tray.) You will be surprised to see your experiment turn into a miniature fireworks display.

Make Paper and Cork Dance under Glass

You will need: A small pane of glass, two books, silk handkerchief, tissue paper, cork, glycerin.

It is surprising to see how easily and quickly a charge of static electricity can be induced in a pane of glass by rubbing it briskly with a silk handkerchief.

Secure the ends of the glass between the pages of two books, raising the glass so that it is about $\frac{3}{4}$ inch from the top of the table. Tear some tissue paper into tiny scraps and spread these out below the glass. Rub vigorously on top of the pane with the piece of silk. Within a few seconds the scraps of tissue paper will appear to "dance" in a lively manner as they are attracted by the static charge of electricity that you are producing in the pane of glass.

A variation of this experiment is to replace the tissue paper with tiny pieces of cork (obtained by cutting and chopping an ordinary bottle cork). These can also be made to "perform" once you have induced a static charge in the pane of glass.

It is possible to produce a sufficiently strong charge of static electricity

Scraps of tissue paper dancing in a lively manner

Scraps of cork can be made to perform, even to produce an initial on the underside of the glass

so that the scraps of cork will hang from the underside of the glass like miniature stalactites.

If you really wish to surprise your friends, however, tell them that the pieces of cork are so obedient that you can make them form the initial of your name.

The secret of this trick is to first have your pane of glass suitably prepared. This is done by smearing an outline of glycerin in the shape of your initial on the *underside* of the glass.

When you now rub the top of the glass with the silk handkerchief, the pieces of cork will be attracted to the underside. Where they come into contact with the glycerin they actually adhere to the glass.

Stop rubbing the glass and the pieces of cork outside the glycerin outline will fall back to the table, leaving your initial clearly "written" in cork chips.

How Water Spurts

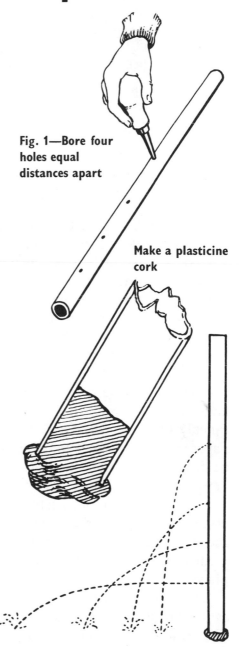

You will need: A length of cardboard tubing, plasticine, water, gimlet.

Take a length of cardboard tubing and use a gimlet to bore four small holes equal distances apart along the side of the tube, as shown in Fig. 1.

Fig. 1—Bore four holes equal distances apart

Use plasticine as a cork at one end of the tube, forcing the plasticine into position so that the joint is water-tight.

Make a plasticine cork

The tube is now ready for your experiment—which will be best performed either in the garden or over a bathtub or large bowl.

Take a large jug of water and fill the tube. Immediately, water will begin to spurt from the four holes. You will find that the holes nearest the top of the tube have the weakest jets. It is the lowest hole, bearing the pressure from the full column of water, which will spurt the farthest.

The lower holes spurt farther than the others

Make Smoke Obey

Fig. 1—Position the cardboard chimneys and draw around them

You will need: A shoe box, two cardboard tubes, razor blades, stub of birthday candle, pencil, scissors, one sheet of paper.

Here is a neat little trick which will help to mystify your non-scientific friends. Perform it on a metal table top.

Find an empty shoe box or similar container that has a lid. Place two small cardboard tubes in position on the lid, as shown in Fig. 1, and draw around them. With the razor blade, cut holes inside the outlines which you have drawn. The two cardboard chimneys should fit tightly into the holes you have made for them. Replace the lid.

Now roll up and twist a small sheet of paper into a match shape, but about twice as large. This is called a paper spill. Light one end and then quickly blow the flame out. Tell your friend to hold the now smoking paper spill to the top of any of the cardboard chimneys. He will probably be disappointed when he obeys you and finds that nothing exceptional happens.

Now remove the lid. Light your little candle and let a few drops of wax fall on a spot in the bottom of the box exactly below one hole. Place the lighted candle on the wax spot so that it stands up and burns immediately under one of the cardboard tubes (Fig. 3) when the lid is replaced.

This time, when a smoking spill of paper is held to the other chimney, as shown in Fig. 4, the smoke will be drawn down into the box and carried up and out through the second tube.

Although this looks quite remarkable when the experiment is successfully performed, the reason is simple. The burning candle quickly consumes all the oxygen in the box and draws in a further supply from the tube farthest away from it, sending the used warm air out through the chimney immediately above it. This is a natural process for a burning flame. The smoke from the paper spill will also be drawn down into the box and will be seen to issue from the other cardboard tube immediately above the candle.

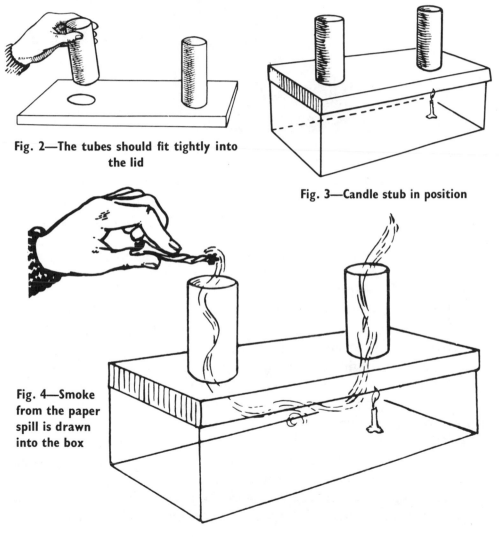

Fig. 2—The tubes should fit tightly into the lid

Fig. 3—Candle stub in position

Fig. 4—Smoke from the paper spill is drawn into the box

Finding the Center of Gravity

You will need: Card, pencil, compass, scissors, thread.

The story is told that while Sir Isaac Newton was in his garden an apple fell on his head from a tree. The great scientist immediately began to wonder what caused the apple to fall while the sun, moon and other stars remained overhead and (fortunately) showed no tendency to follow the apple.

The theory of gravity for which Newton is now famous proves valuable in many aspects of our modern life. Airplanes have to be so constructed and powered that they can sucessfully resist the force of gravity. Cars and trucks, and especially tall vehicles, have to be made with their centers of gravity low enough to withstand any tendency to topple over when driven around sharp corners.

Designers and engineers have to work out complicated mathematical formulae to discover the center of gravity of the product they are working on. Provided we use small objects, such as pieces of a card of different shapes, we can discover their centers of gravity.

For the first experiment draw a small circle with the aid of compass and pencil. Cut this disc out and note that it will balance perfectly when a needle point is placed on the center mark left by the compass.

Similarly, cut out a small square of card and draw diagonal lines from the corners of the square. The spot where the diagonals cross each other

indicates the center of the square. When you place a needle point at this center you find that the square of card will balance perfectly.

The work of finding the center of gravity of an irregularly shaped piece of card becomes somewhat more complicated, however. First suspend the card from one of its corners by a piece of thread tacked to the wall. When it has settled in position take a ruler and continue the line of the thread straight down across the card. Next, suspend the card by another corner. Again, allow the card to become settled and use a ruler to extend the line of the thread across the card.

The center of gravity of the irregularly shaped piece of card occurs where these two diagonals cross each other. Place the card on a needle point at this spot and it will balance perfectly.

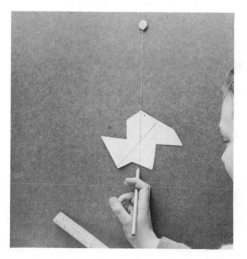

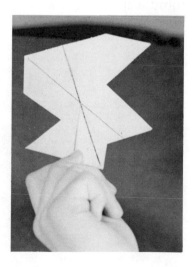

Spaces between Molecules

You will need: Two glasses, cotton, water.

Scientists know that even in solid objects there are many minute spaces between the small particles of matter, which they call "molecules." This simple experiment proves there are spaces. What happens?

Start with the two glasses. Fill one with water, the other with absorbent cotton. The photo above shows the two glasses arranged: one filled with water and the other with cotton.

Now slowly pour the water over the cotton, until one glass successfully holds the contents of both glasses. (See photo below.) Of course you cannot see that the molecules of the water and the wool are now filling the minute spaces that were formerly empty, but you have proved it.

Heat Conductors

Hold a wire to a candle flame—but be ready to drop it quickly!

You will need: Wire, glass rod, wooden rod, candle.

We speak of certain materials as being good conductors of heat and others as poor conductors. By this, we mean that whereas one material will readily absorb and pass heat along its length, another will resist it and try to confine the heat to its source.

An ordinary candle flame will permit us to perform a few simple experiments to show the relative heat conductability of various types of materials.

First, hold a glass rod to a candle flame. No matter how long you keep it there, the end of the rod which you are holding will remain unaffected by the heat at the other end. This is because glass is an extremely poor conductor of heat.

Be careful when you remove the rod from the flame, however. Glass always looks so deceptively cool—and this will not be the case with the end of the rod which has been held to the flame. In fact, it will be uncomfortably hot. So take care.

Now try the same experiment with a wooden rod. The end of this will char and may possibly flame up after it has been held to the candle for a few seconds. The end which you are holding will remain cool because wood is also a poor conductor of heat.

Finally, take a length of wire and hold one end of this in the candle flame. Be prepared to drop the wire suddenly, however, for within a very short time the wire will have conducted heat from the candle flame to your finger tips to an uncomfortable degree.

This will prove that although glass and wood are poor conductors of heat, metal is a good conductor. Perhaps you can answer the following question now: Why do saucepans and kettles have wooden handles?

15

The Candle at the Door

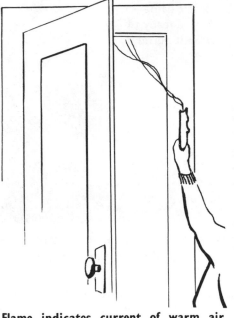

Flame indicates current of warm air leaving the room

You will need: A candle.

Here is a simple test you can make of convection currents at work.

When a room is being heated, the hot air in the room always rises and seeks to escape. Meanwhile, cold air is drawn into the room at a low level to fill the area of low pressure created by the rising warm air.

Allow a room to get thoroughly warm. Then open the door a few inches and hold a lighted candle to the top of the partly-opened door. The direction of the flame will indicate that there is a current of air escaping from the room.

Now hold the candle as low as possible at the door opening. The movement of the flame (plus the cold draft which you will feel) will indicate that there is a current of cold air flowing into the room.

Now experiment with the position of the candle flame about midway between these two extremes of distance. With patience you will find a spot where the flame burns steadily, indicating that there are no drafts at this particular position.

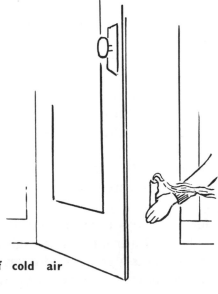

Flame indicates current of cold air entering the room

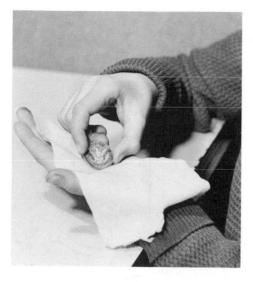 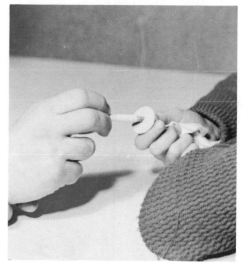

A Trick of Heat

You will need: A quarter (or other coin), handkerchief, wooden skewer or pencil.

Tell your friends that you can hold a piece of burning wood to a handkerchief without scorching or burning the cloth.

(If your mother is not too anxious to see this experiment performed with a good linen handkerchief, let her find you an old piece of linen from her rag bag.)

Place a quarter in the center of the handkerchief and fold the cloth over the coin, twisting the ends together so that the handkerchief is drawn tightly across the face of the coin.

Now place the end of a pencil in the flame of a candle until the wood is glowing red. Press the end of the smoldering wood for 10 seconds against the handkerchief. When the pencil is removed and any loose ash blown away from the cloth there will be no sign of scorching.

This is because the metal coin is such a good conductor of heat that it carries the heat from the end of the smoldering wood right through the handkerchief with such speed that it has no time to scorch the cloth.

The Power in Air Pressure

You will need: Water, a screw-top can, source of heat.

We have seen something of air pressure at work in other experiments in this book. The present experiment shows the quite startling pressure which air can exert under certain circumstances.

You must obtain an empty clean tin can with a well-fitting screw-top that makes it airtight. The larger the can, the more spectacular the experiment will be.

Pour half a cupful of water into the can and then place it (without the screw-top) on a stove and allow the water to boil.

When steam is issuing from the mouth of the can, remove the can from the source of heat and screw the cap tightly into position. (Use a cloth to hold the can.)

As the can cools you will notice that its sides begin to show signs of strain. By the time the can has properly cooled, the sides will be buckled inward to such an extent that you may well be surprised that air pressure alone could have caused the damage.

When the water boiled, the steam and water vapor thus generated forced most of the air out of the can. The screw-top prevented the return of the air and as the can cooled, the steam trapped inside it condensed again into water and thus lowered the pressure inside the can.

We know that air detests vacuums or areas of low pressure and does its best to secure an entry into them. It was the pressure from the outer air as the steam inside the can condensed, which caused the sides of the can to bend inward in such a spectacular manner.

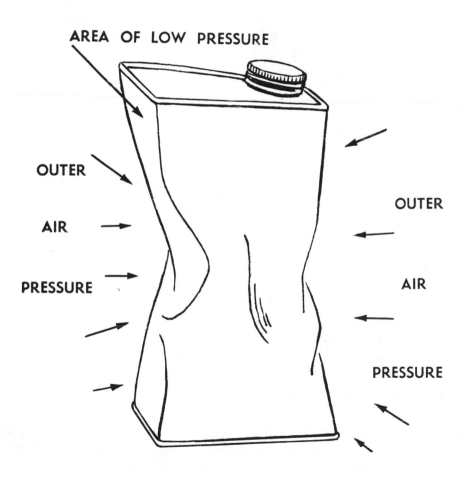

AREA OF LOW PRESSURE

OUTER

AIR

PRESSURE

OUTER

AIR

PRESSURE

Testing the Skin of Water

You will need: Water, water glass, eye-dropper, tissue paper, razor blade, soup plate.

Of course, water has no real "skin" but it does have a tension at the surface that can be readily demonstrated by experiment. For instance, it is possible to overfill an ordinary glass so that the water stands some one-eighth of an inch higher than the edges of the glass.

Take a dry glass and fill it almost to the top with water, taking care that none spills down the sides at this stage. Place the glass in the soup plate and then use the eye-dropper to add further water to the glass until

the level is well above its edges. It is the surface tension of water which allows you to overfill the glass in this fashion.

A further proof of this tension can be obtained by floating a razor blade on water. Place the razor blade on a small piece of tissue paper and float the paper on the surface of the water. After a minute or two the paper will become saturated (i.e., all the air will be driven from the paper and replaced by water) and it will sink to the bottom of the glass leaving the razor blade floating on the surface. You can use a needle in place of the razor blade.

Squeezing the Air

Bring your fist sharply down upon the free end of the ruler

You will need: Newspaper, ruler.

We live in a vast "sea" of air on this planet, and it exerts pressure around us and on our bodies all the time.

Scientists have measured this pressure and find that it amounts approximately to 15 pounds of pressure for every square inch. When you think of the number of square inches over your body you may well wonder why you are able to move around so easily. In fact, it is only possible because our wonderful bodies have been so adjusted that we neither notice this pressure nor suffer any ill effects from it. Indeed, if there were no air we would die.

An easy way of proving the presence of air pressure is to cover a ruler with a large sheet of newspaper so that one end of the ruler projects over the table, as shown in the picture.

Now bring your fist sharply down upon the free end of the ruler. The air pressure on the large area of the newspaper will dislike being squeezed upward so suddenly and it will hold the ruler to the table so that it will resist the blow with your fist. If you strike downward with sufficient force you can even snap the ruler, without tearing the newspaper.

Let Air Show Its Muscles

You will need: A balloon, three or four books.

Have you ever noticed a car with a flat tire? The vehicle is no longer horizontal but sags at that end where the air has been released from the tire.

If you could reach the axle of the car immediately above the flat tire, you would probably find your strength insufficient to raise the end of the car at all.

Yet when air is pumped back into the tire the car is gradually lifted. Air pressure can raise the weight of quite heavy trucks in this fashion.

A similar experiment to test the lifting strength of air pressure can be performed with a toy balloon and a few books. Secure three or four books with rubber bands or string and place them on top of a toy balloon. Place the balloon so that the mouthpiece overhangs the edge of the table.

Take a deep breath and blow steadily into the balloon. You will be surprised to see how easily the end of the pile of books is raised into the air. See if you can lift more books than your friend, in this fashion.

The Expanding Cap

You will need: Food jar and cap.

Have you ever seen your mother struggling to unscrew the metal cap of a jar that refuses to budge? Often, because of the partial vacuum in the jar, and the sticky nature of the contents, caps become quite difficult to remove.

Perhaps you will be able to help.

You have proved that metal is a good conductor of heat, much better than glass. Therefore, if you can contrive to warm the metal cap it should expand more than the jar—and this expansion should be sufficient to enable you to unscrew the cap.

You can either turn the jar upside down in a saucepan and pour about half an inch of hot water into the container, or you can hold the metal cap under a stream of hot water from the faucet for a minute.

You will discover that this will indeed enable you to remove the cap from the jar. Another example of science being put to practical use!

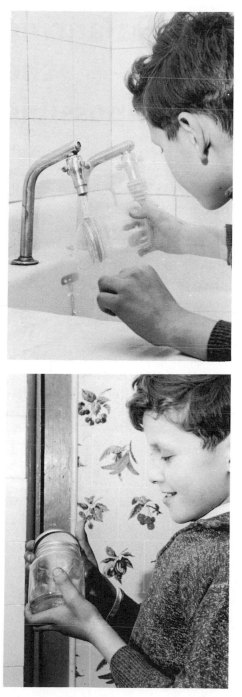

Balancing the Impossible

You will need: Pencil, penknife, hammer, ruler, string 10 inches long, cork, two forks, wooden matchstick, thread.

In a previous experiment we discovered how to find the center of gravity on an irregularly shaped piece of card, and also proved that once we have the center of gravity of an object it becomes easy to balance it.

Some spectacular balancing feats can be performed by making the center of gravity of an object (or group of objects) much lower than usual.

Take a pencil and penknife for your first experiment. Open the penknife halfway and stick the point of the blade into the side of the pencil, leaving room for your finger to support the pencil point, as shown in the picture. With a

little manipulation of the half-opened penknife you will find it possible to balance the pencil on a number of other objects.

For the next part of this experiment take the hammer, ruler, and string. Tie the ends of the string together to form a simple loop and slip this over the ruler and the handle of the hammer. Position the hammer and ruler, as shown in the second picture, and you will astonish your friends by balancing the ruler with its very tip on the edge of a table.

The third experiment is just as spectacular. Cut a V-shaped notch in the end of a matchstick and insert the other end of the matchstick into the bottom of a cork. Now push two forks into the sides of the cork. Make sure that the forks are firmly in position and then place the notched end of the matchstick on a length of thread. The contraption will balance perfectly, and if you hold the stretched thread at an angle, the whole contraption can be made to glide down the thread without losing its balance.

The contraption will glide along the thread

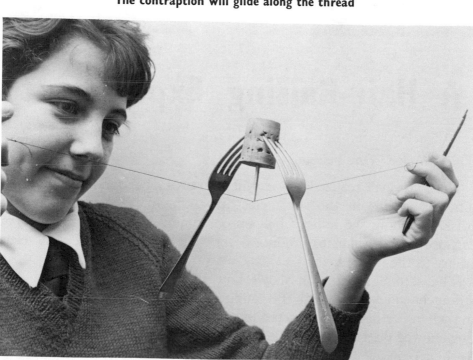

A Hair-Raising Experiment

You will need: One balloon.

Have you ever realized how easy it is to turn a balloon into a magnet? The secret lies in the static electricity which can be generated by briskly rubbing the inflated balloon on some fur or woolen cloth. You can use your sweater to produce a very effective charge of static electricity in the balloon.

The second illustration shows how the balloon attracts hair. And strangely enough, although the young lady said that she could feel nothing when her hair was attracted toward the balloon, both a pet cat and dog showed distinct signs of uneasiness when the balloon was held close to their coats.

Make Your Own Periscope

You will need: Cardboard, two small mirrors, scissors, gummed paper.

Although rays of light travel only in a straight line they can be "bent" or reflected so that images are brought to our view which are normally outside our range of vision.

We cannot normally see around a corner or an open door. But if we hold a mirror at arm's length and so adjust its angle that we can see into it, while at the same time it reflects a view from the other side of the corner or the open door, we have succeeded in "bending" straight lines of light.

If we use two mirrors and employ the double reflection they offer, we can make ourselves a simple periscope. Submarines and tanks use periscopes. These are quite complicated affairs, but still use the same principle of reflecting the rays of light.

You will require cardboard for the casing of your periscope. The width and breadth of this casing will depend upon the sizes of the mirrors you use. The two mirrors cost only a few pennies each and are on sale at large stores as handbag mirrors.

You can make your periscope as tall as you like, always provided the cardboard is stout enough to support the height. The periscope shown in

You can see around a door (or a corner) with the aid of a mirror

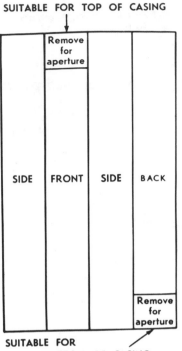

SIDE	FRONT	SIDE	BACK
	Remove for aperture		
			Remove for aperture

SUITABLE FOR
BOTTOM OF CASING

the illustrations is 18 inches tall. Cardboard which was thin enough to cut easily with scissors proved strong enough to make a sturdy little casing of this height.

The sides of your periscope will need to be cut full-length, but the front and the back are shortened to allow for two apertures (openings). The diagram on the left indicates how the pieces of card removed for these apertures are suitable for the top and the bottom of the casing.

Use a strong gummed paper or adhesive tape to join the sides and top of the casing. The viewing apertures must be arranged at opposite ends of the periscope.

When you have completed the casing, secure two pieces of cardboard at angles of 45 degrees with the help of gummed paper. Next comes the important job of fixing the two mirrors in position. These rest on top of

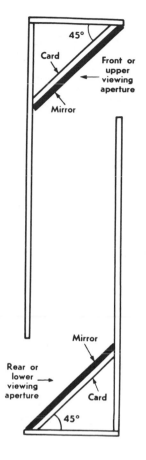

45°

Card

Mirror

← Front or upper viewing aperture

Mirror

Rear or lower → viewing aperture

Card

45°

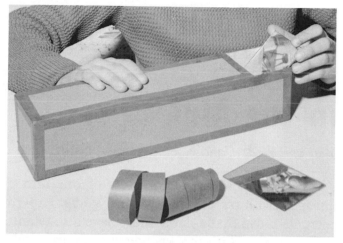

Sliding the mirrors into position

Looking over a wall

the pieces of card which have been previously set at an angle. The photo above shows how to slide one of the mirrors into position. Secure it there with strips of gummed paper.

Once the mirrors have been satisfactorily secured, your periscope is completed. You will be able to have lots of fun looking over walls or around corners. It will also prove useful if you find yourself at the back of a crowd of people when there is a parade or a game taking place.

How Much Oxygen in the Air?

You will need: Candle, empty milk bottle, dish of water.

Air is composed approximately of one-fifth oxygen and four-fifths nitrogen, with traces of a few other gases. Experiments with convection currents prove that a flame must have a constant supply of air if it is to remain alight. With this knowledge, you can find out how much oxygen there is in a milk bottle full of air.

Fill a dish with water, light a stub of candle and carefully float it in the dish. When the flame has established itself and is burning steadily, cover it with the upturned milk bottle.

The candle will continue to burn for a few seconds because it has a small supply of oxygen available in the air now trapped inside the bottle. However, the flame will use this oxygen quite quickly and will then be extinguished. At the same time, because the oxygen content of the bottle has been used, an area of low pressure will result. The outer air, pressing down upon the surface of the water in the dish in its endeavor to enter, will instead, force water up into the bottle, thus indicating the amount of the oxygen which has been used.

Water rises about one-fifth

OUTER AIR

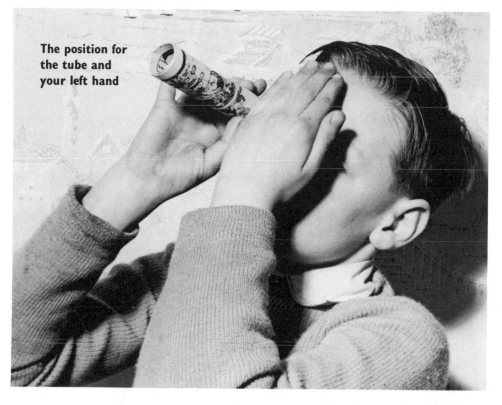

The position for the tube and your left hand

Seeing through a Hole in Your Hand

You will need: Newspaper, scissors, cellophane tape.

It is possible to trick your eyes. But, did you ever realize that it was possible to see through a hole in your hand?

Take a square of newspaper with sides some 9 inches long and roll it into a tube, one inch in diameter. Tape the free end of the paper to the side of the tube.

Take the tube in your right hand and hold it to your right eye so that you can see through it quite clearly.

Now raise your left hand, palm facing you, until it is in front of your left eye with your little finger touching the side of the tube. Open both eyes and look straight ahead. Can you see the hole in your hand?

A Radish Vacuum

You will need: A knife, radish, and saucer.

"Nature abhors a vacuum" and the outer air will always try to enter an area of lower air pressure. This physical law has been put to use many times in various pieces of machinery and equipment.

Possibly the vacuum cleaner is the best known of these machines. Vacuum cleaners may vary in size, shape and performance from maker to maker, but their basic principle is always the same: a vacuum—or at least an area of low pressure—is created by some means (usually electrical). The outer air is then allowed entry in such a manner that it will carry with it any loose dirt, fluff, etc., in its path.

When we press a little rubber suction device to the tiled wall of our bathroom, it is retained in position by air pressure and not by some form of invisible glue.

You can make your own simple form of vacuum sucker from an ordinary radish. Take a large, firm radish and cut it in half with a single stroke of a sharp knife. With the point of the knife scoop out some of the flesh of the radish to form a hollow in that half of the radish which bears the long root.

Now press the half of radish firmly into the center of a clean saucer.

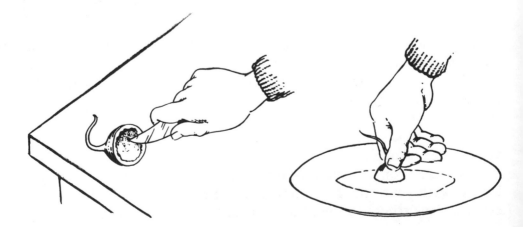

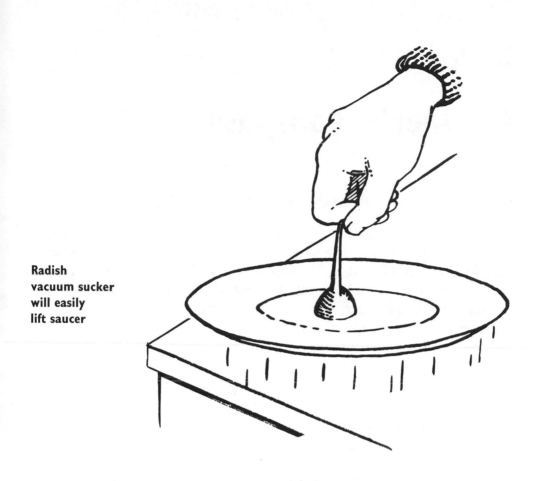

Radish vacuum sucker will easily lift saucer

Lift the radish by its root and you will find that the radish adheres so firmly to the saucer that it raises the plate from the table.

Air pressure is at work, of course. In cutting the radish with a single stroke of the knife you left a clean, flat surface. In scooping out a hollow in the middle of the radish you provided an air space. This air was completely expelled from the hollow when you pressed the radish half firmly against the saucer. The outer air tried to enter the vacuum created in the center of the radish, but the cut surface of the radish had joined in an airtight bond with the saucer. (This bond was further strengthened by juice squeezed from the radish when you exerted pressure to expel the air.) Air was unable to gain entrance and was left pressing down upon the outer surface of the radish, thus "gluing" it to the saucer.

Make a Mariner's Compass

You will need: A needle, cork, knife, small bowl, magnet, water.

Peter Peregrinus was the first man to use a compass. This was in 1269, but even he failed to realize why the compass needle always pointed in one direction. It was left to William Gilbert (1544-1603) to become the first man to realize that the earth itself acted as a huge magnet.

Starting with a magnet, it is possible for you to make a simple form of mariner's compass from ordinary household items.

First, cut a section from the end of a cork. This disk of cork should be about $\frac{1}{2}$ to $\frac{3}{4}$ of an inch thick.

Cutting cork section	**Cutting groove in cork disk**
	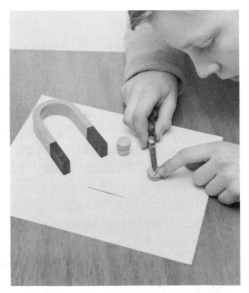

Make a narrow groove in the top of the disk, big enough for a needle to rest firmly in the groove. Use a sharp knife, but be careful not to cut your fingers.

Now comes the task of magnetizing the needle for your compass. Holding the needle at one end between finger and thumb, stroke it 20 times in *one* direction on *one* leg of the magnet. As the needle leaves the magnet at the end of each stroke raise it in a small semicircle above the magnet before commencing the next stroke.

When the needle has been magnetized in this way, place it in the groove on the cork, arranging it so that the needle floats horizontally. Once the cork is placed in a bowl of water you will find that the needle will promptly assume a north-south direction.

(Below) Magnetizing the needle

(Right) The finished compass

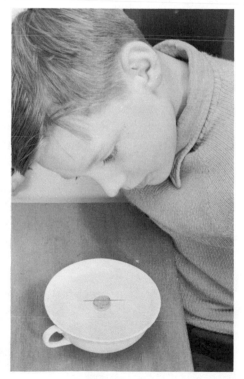

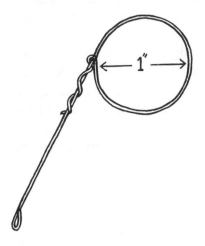

Electrifying a Bubble

You will need: Old phonograph record, piece of fur or flannel, soap, glycerin, wire, paper.

The bubbles for this experiment have a longer life than those usually obtained from ordinary soap solution. The addition of glycerin to soapy water should provide a mixture that will prove ideal for the purpose. If you are unable to get a bubble-pipe, a loop of wire will serve as well.

Take a length of fairly thick wire (hairpin thickness) and bend it into the loop shape shown in the diagram.

Dip the wire loop into the soap and glycerin solution so that a film of liquid forms across the wire when it is removed. Either blow gently into this film or else give the wire a sharp flick in the air to form bubbles.

When you are satisfied with the bubbles you can produce, switch to a second operation: Rub an old phonograph record with a piece of fur or flannel. This is best done in a warm, dry room. Rub the record briskly for a minute or two.

Roll a bubble from the paper to the record

Now, without any loss of time, blow a bubble, catch it on a piece of paper, and then gently roll it onto the phonograph record. A friend can help by blowing a bubble while you are rubbing the record.

Allow the bubble to rest on the record for a few seconds and then gently shake the bubble free. As it falls, lower the record so that it is immediately below the bubble. As the bubble nears the record it will slow in speed until it hovers over it. By careful manipulation of the record, you can keep the bubble in this hovering position either until it bursts or until some wayward current of air blows it aside.

In rubbing the phonograph record you produced an electrical charge which was imparted to the bubble when it rested on the record. As both the record and the bubble were in this way given like charges of electricity, they began to repel each other when the bubble was shaken off.

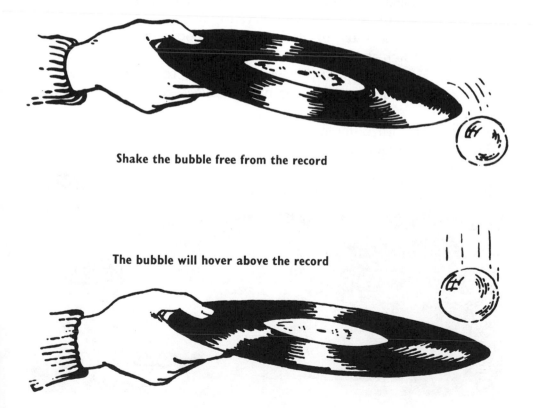

Shake the bubble free from the record

The bubble will hover above the record

How to Reflect Sound

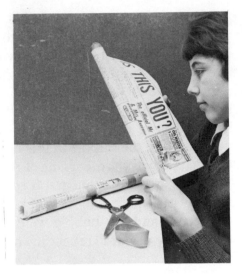

You will need: Newspaper, scissors, gummed cellophane tape, broomstick, watch, cardboard.

Sound waves can be reflected in much the same way that light rays are reflected by a mirror. Make two paper tubes by rolling newspaper around a broomhandle. Tape each tube together.

We do not need a mirror to reflect sound waves. Instead, a sheet of strong cardboard or hardboard will serve to "bounce" them.

The ticking of a watch or clock makes a good sound to experiment with. Hold a watch at one end of a paper tube as you direct it toward the cardboard. Have your partner cover one ear so that she can hear the ticking through the second paper tube, directed toward the sounding board.

Experiment with different positions of the tubes and you will soon appreciate how readily sound waves can be reflected.

A Path for Sound

You will need: Thread, spoons, fork, small cans, water glass.

Strike the end of a fork on the table and perhaps, very faintly, you may hear a noise like a tuning fork. Strike the fork a second time, however, and quickly touch the handle to an empty water glass, and the sound will be magnified.

When you drop something on the floor, the noise it makes must pass through the air to reach your ears, and some sound waves will never reach you.

Tie a fork to the center of a length of thread. Hold the ends of the thread to your ears and lean forward from the waist so that the fork swings freely in front of you. Let a friend strike sharply at the fork with another fork or spoon. The noise produced will travel along the thread and you will hear it quite loudly.

What do you hear?

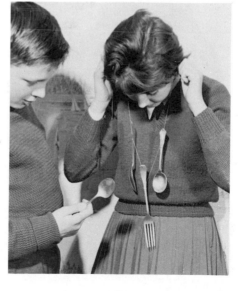

Now tie a spoon on each side of the fork. This time, when the spoons and fork are struck you will hear a pleasing sound resembling a peal of bells.

Try suspending small tin cans and other metal objects from the thread. Strike first one, then another, then all together. What noises do you hear?

A LONGER Path

You will need: Two wooden matchbox trays, thread, wooden matchsticks, scissors, nail.

Use two strongly made matchbox trays and make a small hole in the bottom of each with a nail. Pass one end of a long length of strong thread through one of the holes and tie a matchstick to the end of the thread

so that it is inside the tray. Repeat this with another matchbox tray and matchstick on the other end of the same thread. Pull gently, but firmly, on the matchbox trays so that both matchsticks are tight on the inside of the trays.

Let a friend take one tray while you hold the other. Walk apart so

for Sound

that the thread is taut—but do not pull so hard that the bottoms of the trays are wrenched loose. You must also ensure that nothing is touching the length of thread.

Speak into the tray. Your voice will travel along the path formed by the thread and will be heard quite plainly by your friend at the other end.

You must, of course, use the trays in turn, first as earphones and then as mouthpieces to speak into. If you stretch a long thread out in the garden you will be surprised to find how clearly your voice will carry. But again, take care that nothing (not even a twig or leaf) touches the thread.

41

Make a Boomerang

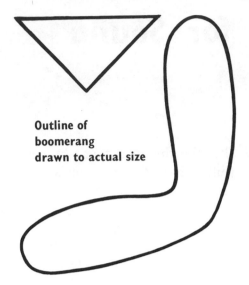

**Outline of
boomerang
drawn to actual size**

You will need: Card, scissors, pencil.

When you make a paper airplane and glide it across the room you are making use of a condition known as "passive flight."

Man had to gain a knowledge of "active flight," however, before he could produce airplanes. One of the earliest forms of active flight is the boomerang used by the aborigines of Australia, and we can observe this in action.

The chief characteristic of this weapon is its ability to return to the thrower. A working boomerang can easily be cut from cardboard. Draw the outline of a small boomerang on a piece of thin cardboard, copying the diagram.

Cut your boomerang out and then balance it on your left fore-finger. Flick one of the legs of the boomerang sharply with your other forefinger. It will take off and revolve through the air like a small propeller before returning to you.

Now try the same experiment with a small triangle of card cut to the size shown. Cut another triangle twice as large as the first and note what difference there is in its active flight compared with that of the small triangle.

How Hot Water Rises

You will need: Two milk bottles, ink, hot and cold water, cardboard.

When you turn on the hot water in the bathroom, do you ever wonder how the hot water got upstairs when the source of heat for warming the water is downstairs?

The reason is that hot water rises —a fact which heating engineers and plumbers make use of. A simple experiment will provide proof enough.

Fill a milk bottle with cold water and cover the top with a square of cardboard. Fill a second milk bottle with hot water to which some ink has been added. Both bottles should be filled to the brim.

Carefully upturn the bottle containing the cold water, holding the square of cardboard across the neck as a simple cork. Position it immediately above the bottle containing the hot water.

Holding both bottles steady, slip the piece of card out from between them and watch what happens. The colored hot water will rise up into the bottle containing the cold water, while the cold water will sink into the lower bottle.

(Above) Cold water positioned above hot water

(Below) Hot water and cold water changing places

43

Water Expands When It Freezes

You will need: Water, empty screw-cap medicine or ketchup bottle, plastic water tumbler.

When water freezes it occupies a larger volume (space) than in its fluid state. This is easily proved by simple experiment, carried out on a cold winter's night, or in your home freezer.

Take an empty bottle with a screw cap. Fill the bottle to the very top with water and then screw the cap tightly. If the temperature is below freezing, place the filled bottle outdoors in an exposed position before you go to bed. If not, place it in a loose cardboard box in your freezer, but be sure it is standing up.

When the water freezes, the ice will break the bottle

When the water in the bottle turns into ice, what will happen ? Because ice requires more space than water, and because the screw cap will not allow this increase in space, the sides of the bottle will crack open. (Be very careful with the broken glass!)

For another proof, take a plastic tumbler instead of an empty bottle and fill the tumbler to the brim with water.

Now place the filled tumbler in the freezing compartment of your kitchen refrigerator and allow sufficient time for the water to freeze solid. You will find that the level of the ice is much higher than the brim.

Make a Simple Siphon

You will need: Length of rubber tubing, two large jars.

This is an extremely simple experiment, yet one that often has practical value when it becomes necessary to empty a receptacle of liquid, especially to make it rise over an obstruction.

When you drink lemonade through a straw, you are making the liquid overcome the force of gravity. You first suck all the air from the straw, which allows the outer air to press down upon the surface of the lemonade and assist it in its journey from the glass to your mouth.

With a siphon, you do the same thing—empty a glass of water—or just as easily, a large tank containing many gallons.

To make a siphon, fill an empty jar with clean water and insert one end of the tubing into the jar. Arrange a second jar at a lower level within easy reach of the other end of the tubing.

Suck the free end of the tube until you have removed all the air and the tube is filled with water. Remove the end of the tube carefully from your mouth, holding a finger tightly over the end as your tongue lets go, so that suction is maintained.

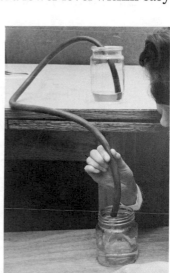

Place the end of the tubing in the empty jar and remove your finger from the end. The water will flow steadily now from the top jar into the bottom one for as long as you can keep the top end of the tube below the surface of the water you are emptying.

How to "Kill" a Potato

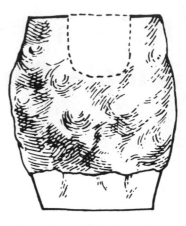

Fig. 1

You will need: Two potatoes, knife, sugar, dish of water.

Take two potatoes of roughly equal size and "kill" one of them by boiling it for 20 minutes. Now slice the top and bottom off both potatoes and scoop a hollow in each. Then remove a complete circle of peel from the lower half of each potato (Fig. 1).

Place a spoonful of granulated sugar in the cavity of each potato. Fill a dish with water and stand the two potatoes in the water.

Leave the potatoes 24 hours. At the end of this time the cavity in the raw potato will be full of water and sugar, but the sugar in the cooked potato will be undisturbed.

This drawing up of water by the living cells of a plant is called "osmosis." By cooking the second potato we "killed" the cells and thus prevented osmosis from taking place.

Cavity filled with water and sugar in the raw potato

Sugar remains unaffected in the cooked potato

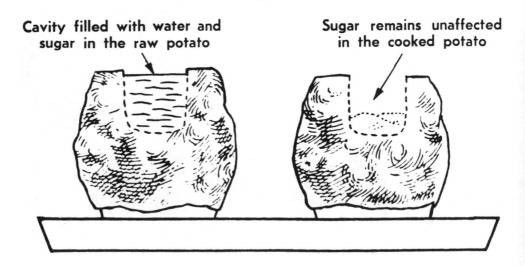

A Lively Celluloid Fish

You will need: Scissors, celluloid or sheet plastic.

Cut a simple fish shape about 4 inches in length from a piece of celluloid or sheet plastic. Give your fish a fairly large tail, as shown below.

Tell your friend about the lifelike properties of this toy fish—how it will curl and wriggle in a friendly manner when placed in the palm of a warm hand.

Let your friend rub his hands together for a moment or two, so that they are really warm. Get him to extend one hand, palm uppermost, and place the fish in position. Within a few seconds the fish will be curling its head and tail up to meet each other.

The reason for this display of agility is the fact that the plastic does not become warm evenly. The underside expands as it is warmed by the palm of your friend's hand, but the cold upper surface remains the same. The expansion of the underside forces the toy fish to curl quite vigorously.

(Left) Cut a simple fish shape

(Below) The expanded underside causes the fish to curl

47

Make a Simple Electric Motor

You will need: A large cork, plastic knitting needle, covered wire, 6-volt battery with lead-in wires, plywood, tin can, adhesive tape, magnet, tin-snips, pliers, hammer, U-shaped brads, nails, screws.

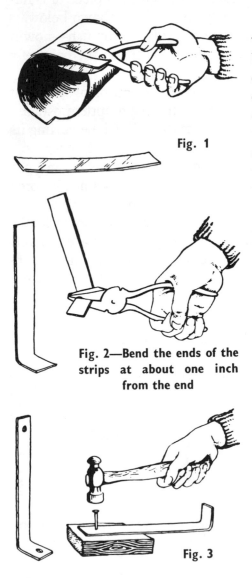

Fig. 1

Fig. 2—Bend the ends of the strips at about one inch from the end

Fig. 3

Michael Faraday was the first man who succeeded in driving a machine by electricity. This was in 1821. His experiments paved the way for the enormous use of electric power in domestic and industrial work today.

With quite simple materials we can make a small electric motor which can safely be driven by a 6-volt battery.

First, cut two strips of metal from an empty tin can with the snips—taking care not to cut yourself. The strips should be about 5 inches long by $5\frac{3}{4}$ inches wide. Bend the ends of these strips over with the pliers at about one inch from the end.

Fig. 4—Position the metal strips so that they can receive a plastic knitting needle

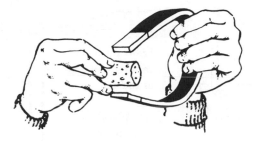

Fig. 5—Choose a cork which fits easily between the legs of a magnet

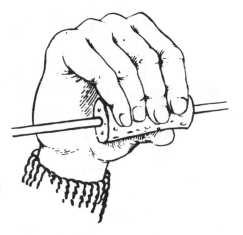

Fig. 6—Push the knitting needle through the center of the cork

Use a hammer and a sharp nail to make a hole in each end of each metal strip, as shown in Fig. 3, and screw them to a small plywood base-board. Adjust the distance between the strips so that a plastic knitting needle can be housed in the holes at the top (see Fig. 4).

Make sure that the knitting needle revolves quite freely in its metal housing. Select a large cork that will fit easily between the ends of the magnet, and then skewer the cork on the knitting needle (Fig. 6). Nail 2 U-shaped brads into the base.

Take 40 or 50 turns of covered wire around the cork to form a coil, as shown in Fig. 7.

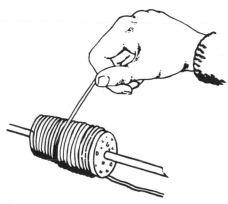

Fig. 7—Take 40 or 50 turns of wire around the cork

Now remove the insulation from the two free ends of the wire leading from the coil. Use adhesive tape to secure the ends of the wire to oppo-site sides of the knitting needle, but be sure that the bared ends of the wire are not covered by the tape or touching each other.

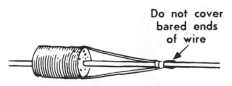

Do not cover bared ends of wire

Fig. 8—Secure the ends of the wire with adhesive tape to opposite sides of the needle

49

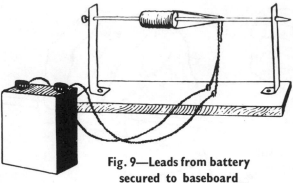

Fig. 9—Leads from battery
secured to baseboard

Leads must make contact with ends of the coil

Fig. 10—Ends of leads must make contact with ends of wire from coil

Note the set-up in Fig. 9, and start by attaching the lead-in wires to the bared ends of the wired coil before attaching them to the battery posts. In fact, put them through the brads first also, so that they will not get tangled. The ends of the lead-in wires must be bared to make contact.

Now hold the magnet in position so that the coil can revolve freely between the ends of the magnet legs without actually touching them. Give the cork a spin with your finger and the motor will start up and spin by itself while you hold the magnet there.

Should the knitting needle spindle have a tendency to work free from the metal housing, impale a small cork on the pointed end of the needle to retain it in position (see Fig. 11).

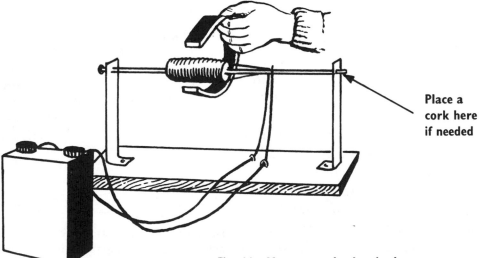

Place a cork here if needed

Fig. 11—Motor completely wired up

Sympathetic Vibrations

You will need: Two glasses, fine wire, water, pencil.

Pour water into a glass until it is about a third full. Tap the glass with a pencil and it will give out a musical note. Add a little more water and the note will change in tone. Fill the glass to the brim with water and tap it again—yet a different note will result. The tapping causes the sides of the glass to vibrate and make sound.

Let us return to the beginning—with our glass about one-third full of water. Take a second glass and pour a similar quantity of water into this. Tap the first glass, remember the note it gives out, and quickly tap the second glass. If there is any difference in the two notes, add water to one of the glasses until they both emit the same note when struck lightly with the pencil.

Stand the glasses about 4 or 5 inches apart and place a piece of fine wire across the top of the glass that is farthest from you. Now strike the nearest glass and you will see a slight movement of the wire on the other glass.

The wire responds to your tapping of the other glass because both glasses vibrate in sympathy. If you have adjusted the water content of each so that they emit identical notes, you will be able to make the wire on the first glass gradually move to the edge and finally fall, by tapping with your pencil on the second glass.

Sympathetic
vibrations
will cause the
wire to fall

Propelling a Toy Boat with Detergent

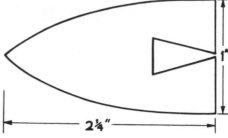

You will need: Card, scissors, pencil, large plate or bowl, water, screwdriver, detergent.

In this experiment we will try to lessen the surface tension of water at a certain area, and see what effect it has.

First, draw a simple boat shape on a piece of card, to the dimensions indicated in the diagram. Cut this out carefully, including the triangle.

Fill a large plate with water and launch your boat to make sure it floats well.

Now take a little detergent powder on the blade of a screwdriver or the end of a knife, and drop it carefully into the small, triangular opening that you have cut in the stern of your small boat.

Within a few seconds the boat will be traveling forward through the water, as the detergent breaks down the surface tension and tries to expand through the narrow opening in the rear of the model.

Try repeating this experiment, with a drop of oil from an oil can, in place of the detergent, or by floating a small piece of camphor at the rear of the model boat. Both oil and camphor have an effect on surface tension, as you will notice.

The Three-Part Candle Flame

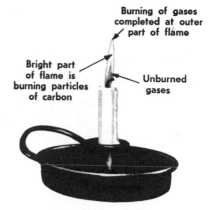

Burning of gases completed at outer part of flame

Bright part of flame is burning particles of carbon

Unburned gases

You will need: Candle, piece of cardboard.

Light a candle and when the flame is burning steadily study it carefully. It consists of three parts. In the center is a bluish area which contains the unburned gases from the candle wax. Surrounding this center area is the brightest part of the flame. This is composed of burning particles of carbon which give most of the light from the flame. Outside these two parts of the flame is a fainter area where the burning of the gases is completed.

With care, you can produce proof of these three parts of a candle flame. Cut a piece of white cardboard and hold it steadily in a candle flame for 3 or 4 seconds (but not long enough for the card to catch on fire). At the end of this time, lift the card quickly away from the flame.

The photograph on the right shows you the type of mark which the flame will leave on the card if the experiment is performed carefully. The inside area of the flame consisting of the unburned gases will leave the card unmarked. The burning particles of carbon will leave a deposit of soot. And the outer area of the flame will leave a fine scorch mark.

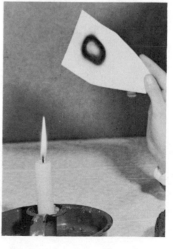

Holding card in candle flame

(Right) Proof on the card

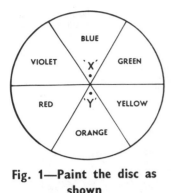

Fig. 1—Paint the disc as shown

All Colors Produce White

You will need: Card, pencil, scissors, water-color paints, brush, string or thread, compass.

The first man to discover that ordinary white daylight was really a combination of bright colors was Sir Isaac Newton, a modest, scientific genius born in 1642. It was while he was experimenting with telescopes that he first noticed the colors of the spectrum—the same colors which we see in a rainbow.

He discovered that a ray of light entering his darkened laboratory, when reflected through a prism, was split up into these colors and therefore rightly thought that they produced white light.

There is a simple experiment which will enable us to test this for ourselves.

Set your compass at 1½ inch radius and draw a circle on a piece of cardboard. Keep the compass at the same measurement and use it to mark

Fig. 2—Painting the spectrum

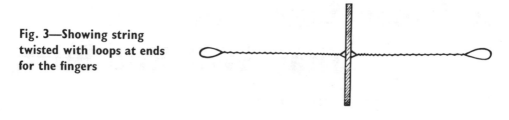

Fig. 3—Showing string
twisted with loops at ends
for the fingers

off six equal divisions around the circle. Draw straight lines from these points at the outside directly to the center of the circle, as in Fig. 1.

Paint the various sections of the cardboard disc the colors marked. Ordinary watercolors from your paint box will serve quite well for this.

Allow time for the paint to dry and then make two small holes near the center of the disc, about $\frac{1}{2}$-inch apart (see X and Y).

Now pass a piece of thread about $3\frac{1}{2}$ feet in length through the two holes in the middle of the disc (Fig. 3), and tie the two ends together.

Hold the string by the loops at each end and get a friend to slide the cardboard disc along until it is midway between your hands. Now twirl the disc around until the string is tightly twisted and pull gently on the loops. You will soon find it quite easy to keep the disc spinning at high speed.

Once the card is spinning around really fast you will find that the bright colors you have painted on it merge together to produce white.

Fig. 4—All you see
is white

A Paper Saucepan
That Will Not Burn

You will need: Paper, pencil, scissors, paper clips, water, candle.

As we know, some materials are good conductors and others are poor conductors of heat. Most of our cooking utensils are made of metals because they are such good conductors and therefore cook our food and

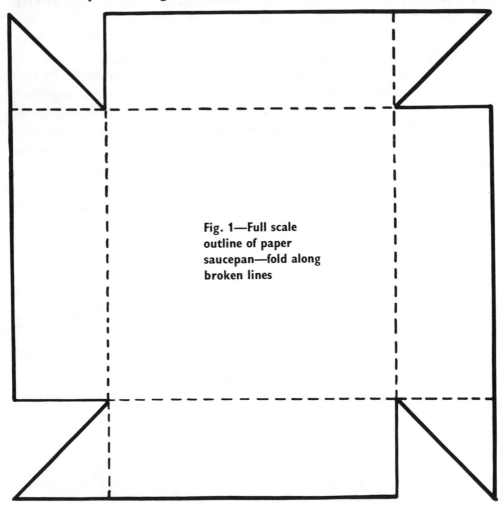

Fig. 1—Full scale
outline of paper
saucepan—fold along
broken lines

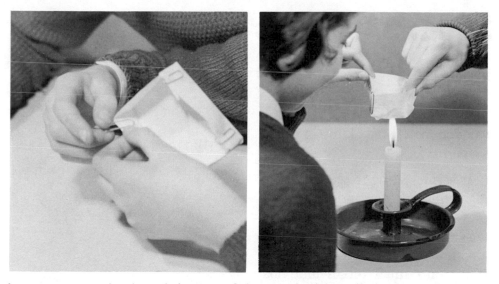

heat our water in the minimum of time and with as little expenditure of heat as possible.

What happens when we use material that is a bad conductor of heat for our saucepan? We will use ordinary drawing paper, and see what happens.

Fig. 1 gives the full-size outline for a simply made paper saucepan. Trace this outline and transfer it to your drawing paper. Cut around the outline and fold along the dotted lines, as shown.

Use paper clips to secure the four corners of the saucepan.

Half fill the saucepan with water and make quite sure that you have a water-tight little container. Light a candle and carefully hold the paper saucepan over the flame. Be careful not to burn yourself. It is best to have a friend hold one side of the little paper container.

You will be surprised to find that although you hold the saucepan in the flame for a minute or two, the paper will not catch on fire.

When you finally remove the saucepan the water it contains will be quite warm, but apart from a circle of soot on the underside of the container the paper will probably be unharmed.

The reason for this is that the water inside the container is a remarkably good conductor of heat, while the paper is a bad conductor. As a result, the water carried the heat away from the underside of the paper so quickly that it had no time to scorch or burn the paper.

Sugar Attracts Water, Soap Repels Water

You will need: Bowl of water, wooden matchstick, lump of sugar, soap.

It is interesting to see the differing actions of soap and sugar when they are allowed to touch the surface of a bowl of water.

Cut a wooden splinter (or matchstick) into small pieces and float them on the surface of the water. When a cube of sugar is placed in the center of the water (see Fig. 1) the pieces of wood are immediately attracted toward it. This does not occur because the sugar has suddenly developed any magnetic tendencies, but because the sugar is so porous that it draws water into it-

Fig. 1

self. The pieces of wood can be seen moving toward the sugar on the small current which has been created.

If you replace the sugar with a small sliver of soap you will see the reverse action. The soap gives off a slight, oily film which spreads quickly outward from the point where the soap touches the water and weakens the surface tension. The pieces of wood are similarly affected and their movement is also outward and away from the piece of soap.

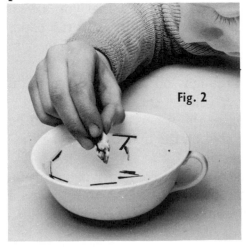

Fig. 2

Miniature Iceberg

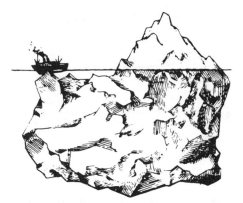

You will need: Bowl of water, plastic mug.

Many ships have been wrecked by icebergs which drift southward from the Arctic regions. Icebergs are huge, floating islands of ice which present a great threat to shipping.

Because of the relative density of ice and water, some seven-eighths of an iceberg is beneath the surface as it floats and only one-eighth can be seen above the surface. A ship can be hundreds of feet away from the visible part of an iceberg and still

From a ship you cannot see all the iceberg

run against ice below the surface as shown above.

Test this for yourself by filling a plastic cup with water and freezing it solid in the refrigerator. Remove the cup and allow warm water to run over the outside for a few moments. This will loosen the block of ice and enable you to remove it.

Fill a bowl with water and float the ice in the bowl. You will quickly see how much of the ice is below the surface when your miniature iceberg is floating.

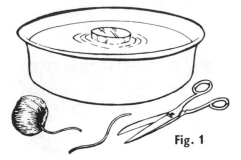

Fig. 1

Ice on a String

You will need: Ice, bowl of water, string, salt, spoon.

Put salt on the ice around the string

Fig. 2

Fig. 3—When the ice freezes again it will trap the end of the string

While you still have the ice block from the previous experiment, try this trick on your friends.

Keep the ice floating in the bowl of water and cut a short length of string, some 6 or 7 inches long.

Ask your friend if he can lift the ice from the water with the aid of the string.

When he finally admits himself defeated, show him how this may be done.

Moisten one end of the piece of string and place it on top of the ice. Sprinkle a spoonful of salt over it, as shown in Fig. 2. The salt will melt the ice around the string, but after a time the ice will freeze over again, this time trapping the end of the string.

By pulling gently on the string you will be able to lift the block of ice clear of the water.

Carry a Column of Water

You will need: Glass of water, drinking straw.

Air pressure is used in many ways for pumping and moving water. Here is a means of moving a column of water.

Place a drinking straw in a glass of water and suck at the straw. First, you remove the air, and air pressure then forces water up in the straw. When water has reached your mouth, place a finger on the top end of the straw as you remove it from your mouth.

Keeping your finger in position, raise the straw from the glass. Trapped inside the straw, and retained there by air pressure, will be a slender column of water.

Release your finger from the end of the straw, thus allowing air to reach the top of the column, and the water will run from the straw.

Make sure that the glass is in correct position to receive the falling column of water.

Your Magic Finger

You will need: Tin can with tight-fitting lid, water, pitcher, gimlet, bowl.

You can use the knowledge gained in the previous experiment with the drinking straw to help mystify your friends. Tell them about your "magic finger." No matter how many holes you make in the bottom of a tin can you can still make it hold water—with the aid of your magic finger!

You will need a sharp gimlet to bore the necessary holes in the can. Start by making a hole in the lid of the can. Make three or four holes in the bottom, too—or better still, let your friend make the holes for you, so that he can see there is no trickery involved.

Hold the can over an empty bowl and pour water into it. Water will

As you try to fill the can the water will pour through the holes in the bottom

immediately begin to stream through the holes you have punched in the bottom. Perhaps your friend would like to try stopping this flow of water. There is not much chance of his success, unless he has seen the experiment before.

To perform the operation successfully yourself, you must fill the can with water, press the lid tightly and quickly into position, and place your finger over the hole in the lid. Immediately, you stop air from entering the top of the can and the outer air presses upward on the under-side of the can to prevent the water from running out.

You will be able to control the flow of the water from the can. Cover the hole in the lid with your finger and the flow will stop. Release your finger and the water will again pour from the bottom of the can.

With the lid on and your finger over the hole, the water remains in the can

As soon as your finger uncovers the hole, the water starts to run out again

Make Water Denser

You will need: Fresh egg, jug, water, salt.

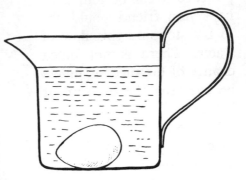

As we have seen in a previous experiment, although ice and water are really the same, they have such different densities that ice will float in water. Here is an experiment which shows you how it is possible to increase the density of water and thereby improve its floating powers.

A new-laid egg sinks in fresh water

Place a fresh egg in a jug of clean water and the egg will sink to the bottom. In fact, your mother knows that this is one way of testing an egg to see if it is fresh, without having to open it.

Stir salt into the jug of water (about an eggcupful of salt to half a pint of water). Replace the egg and this time it will float because you have increased the density of the water.

If you still have your block of ice intact, float this in the salt water and you will notice that more of the ice shows above the brine than when it floated in fresh water.

If you are a swimmer, you have noticed how much easier it is to swim in the sea—provided it is calm—than in fresh water. Why should this be?

The same egg
will float
in salt water

Blowing the Air Away

You will need: Paper, scissors.

Although we cannot see the air which surrounds us it is possible to feel it. Clap your hands in front of your face and you will feel a slight gust of wind. This is the air which has been displaced by bringing your hands sharply together.

Another way of removing air is by blowing it out of the way. This can be done in the following manner.

Cut two strips of paper. Take a piece in each hand and hold them both in front of you so that they are about 5 or 6 inches apart. Now blow steadily between the two sheets of paper.

You may think that by blowing in this fashion you will send the strips of paper farther apart. This will not be so. As you blow between them, the two pieces of paper will move in toward each other until they almost touch.

This is because your action of blowing has removed some of the air between the strips of paper thus causing an area of low pressure at this place. As a result, the outer air forces the strips of paper together.

Rust Uses Up Oxygen

You will need: Steel wool, pencil, rubber band, water glass, dish of water.

Burning and breathing are not the only means of using oxygen from the air. Whenever iron rusts, oxygen is used up in the process.

We can prove this by a simple experiment, but one which is going to need some time. Moisten some steel wool in water and secure it to the top of a pencil with a rubber band, as shown in Fig. 1. Fill a dish with water and arrange the pencil and steel wool inside an up-turned glass (Fig. 2).

Place the dish and its contents in a safe place and leave it for several days. After a sufficient lapse of time you will find that the steel wool has begun to rust. In doing so it will

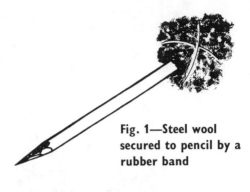

Fig. 1—Steel wool secured to pencil by a rubber band

have used up oxygen from the air in the glass. Also the outer air will have forced up the level of the water inside the glass to offset the area of low pressure caused by the rusting of the metal. When all the oxygen has been used, the water will have risen to about one-fifth of the volume of the water glass.

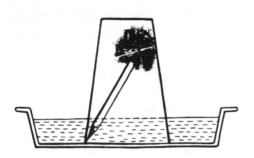

Fig. 2—Glass upturned over steel wool and pencil, in a dish of water

Fig. 3—The rusting metal will slowly use up the oxygen and the level of the water will rise inside the glass

Make Your Own Rain

Rain is forming on the ladle

You will need: Soup ladle, kettle.

Did you ever realize what a simple matter it is to produce rain in your own kitchen?

Take a kettle of water and bring it to a boil. Once the kettle has been heated sufficiently you will notice vapor coming from the spout, indicating that the water inside is boiling. Often, we mistakenly refer to this as "steam," but it cannot be because real steam is invisible.

It is, in fact, water vapor and if you study it carefully you will notice that the vapor does not appear to issue directly from the spout. There is a short distance between the end of the spout and the point where the vapor can first be seen. This seemingly "empty" area is where the actual steam is invisibly leaving the kettle. It quickly cools upon contact with the outside air and becomes the water vapor which we can see.

Water vapor is contained in the clouds which produce our rain. The sun evaporates water from the sea, lakes and rivers, and causes clouds to form. When the clouds are sufficiently cooled they become water again and fall back to earth in the shape of rain (or snow).

You can turn the water vapor from the boiling kettle back into water, simply by cooling it. Allow a soup ladle to stand in cold water until it is thoroughly chilled. Dry the ladle so that no water remains upon it.

Hold the ladle carefully by its handle and arrange the metal bowl of the ladle to come into contact with the stream of water vapor issuing from the kettle. Within a few seconds the vapor will condense on the cold metal and drops of water will fall from the end of the ladle. This is rain.

Air Presses in all Directions

You will need: A jar, balloon.

When we speak about air pressure, we are often mistaken in thinking that it presses in only one direction at a time. This, of course, is not so. Air exerts its force in all directions. Only when a vacuum or an area of low pressure is created does air appear to marshal its forces and move in the direction necessary to increase the pressure in that area.

A simple experiment will prove the point.

Even a partially-inflated balloon will lift the jar

Take an ordinary rubber balloon and hold it so that it hangs partially in an empty jar.

As you blow into the balloon and inflate it, that part of the balloon which is trapped in the jar swells out until it touches the glass sides. A few more puffs, and it becomes an easy matter to lift the jar with the aid of the balloon.

The air pressure inside the balloon exerts its force in all directions, pressing the walls of the balloon so tightly against the glass jar that it cannot easily be pulled free unless some air is released from the balloon.

Make a Pinhole Camera

Fig. 1—Check the box and lid for any leaks of light

You will need: Small cardboard box, ruler, pencil, scissors, razor blade, compass, gummed paper, greaseproof paper or tracing paper, candle.

Here is an interesting experiment which will give endless fun. You need a small cardboard box for the body of your camera. Choose one with a nice, deep lid.

First, hold both the box and the lid up to a bright light, as in Fig. 1. Mark any places where you can see even a pinpoint of light.

The box used here had battered corners and these allowed a considerable amount of light to leak through. All these weak points were covered with brown gummed paper (Fig. 2) until no more light could be seen through them.

When satisfied that your box is completely lightproof, draw two diagonals to find the center point of the lid. Use a compass to make a clean hole through the center point, as shown in Fig. 3.

A rectangular hole (aperture), measuring about $2\frac{1}{2}$ inches by $1\frac{1}{2}$ inches must now be cut from the bottom of the box. Mark the best

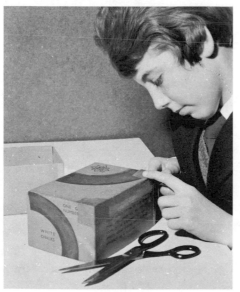

Fig. 2—Patch up any weak spots

MAKE A PINHOLE CAMERA
(continued)

position in the center of the box, and then carefully remove the piece of cardboard, with the aid of ruler and razor blade (Fig. 4).

Now place a screen of fine grease-proof paper over the "window" in the bottom of the box. Use the finest tracing paper or greaseproof paper that you can obtain, as this will provide the best results. Secure the screen with strips of gummed paper, as in Fig. 5.

Your pinhole camera is now complete. Slip the lid into position on the box.

Fig. 3—Use compass point to make hole in center of lid

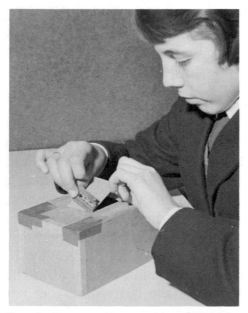

Fig. 4—Remove the aperture from the back of the camera

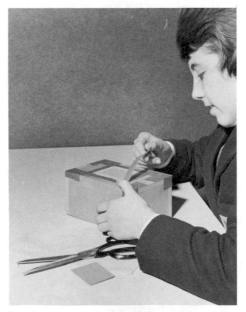

Fig. 5—Secure the tracing paper screen into position

Place a lighted candle a few inches away from the front of the camera, in a darkened room. An image of the candle will appear in an inverted position on the greaseproof screen. By sliding the box in or out of the lid this image can be made larger or smaller.

Aim the camera at the electric light in a room and an inverted image of this will appear on the screen. Focus the camera on the window of your room on a sunny day and the window will appear on your screen —but it will appear upside down.

The reason for this reversal of image is shown in Fig. 7. The rays of light carrying the picture of the subject through the pinhole to the screen travel in straight lines.

This camera, of course, has no film and will not give you any prints.

Fig. 6—Image of candle is inverted on the screen

Fig. 7—Straight rays of light pass through pinhole and invert the image

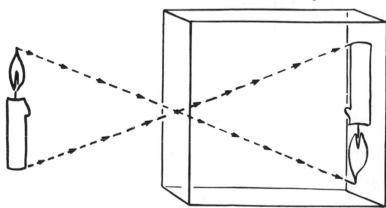

Balloon in a Bottle

You will need: A balloon, two glass tubes, rubber band, bottle or large jar and cork.

Secure a balloon to the end of a glass tube with a rubber band, as illustrated.

Now take a bottle or large jar with a tight-fitting cork. Drill two holes through the cork and insert the tubes (A and B).

A smear of butter on each length of tubing will assist their entry into the cork and also ensure an airtight fit. Another smear of butter around the cork will similarly ensure an airtight fit in the mouth of the jar.

Place the end of tube A in your mouth and suck the air from the jar. As the air is withdrawn you will see the balloon steadily swell. The outer air entering tube B inflates the balloon as it tries to maintain the pressure of air inside the jar.

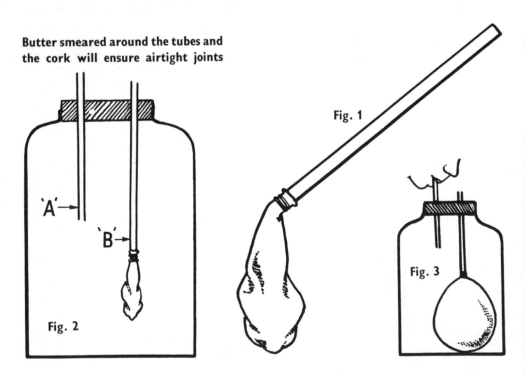

Butter smeared around the tubes and the cork will ensure airtight joints

'A'→

'B'→

Fig. 1

Fig. 2

Fig. 3

Make a Razor Blade Climb

The magnet will not lift the apple

You will need: Magnet, razor blade, card, apple, an assortment of small articles.

To test the powers of a magnet, spread an assortment of small articles on the table. Include an apple.

First try out the magnet on the apple. You will quickly discover that it will not attract fruit. Nor will it attract wood, glass, chalk, cardboard, cloth, or rubber.

You can lift a string of steel items

You will soon discover, however, that things made from iron and steel, such as a key, razor blade and nail are not only attracted to the magnet, but also attract each other while under the magnet's influence.

Now take a sheet of thin card and using the magnet as in the photo, make a razor blade climb up the piece of card while it is sloping steeply.

Push a nail into the top of the apple so that it looks like a metal stalk. Now the magnet will be able to lift the apple from the table.

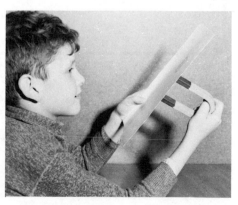

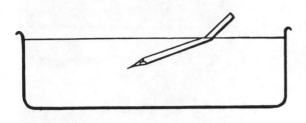

Penny in a Bowl

You will need: Pencil, penny, bowl, water.

When rays of light enter another transparent substance they appear to bend, and this is called refraction.

You can see refraction at work if you dip a pencil into a bowl of water. Only immerse part of the pencil and you will notice that the pencil seems to bend.

Use refraction to play this trick on a friend. Seat him at the table and place a penny in a solid empty bowl so that it is just out of his view, hidden by the rim of the bowl.

Tell your friend that you can bring the penny into view without his moving and without moving the bowl or the coin. Pour water gently into the bowl, so that the coin is not disturbed. As the bowl fills, the refracted rays of light will gradually make the penny appear to float into view.

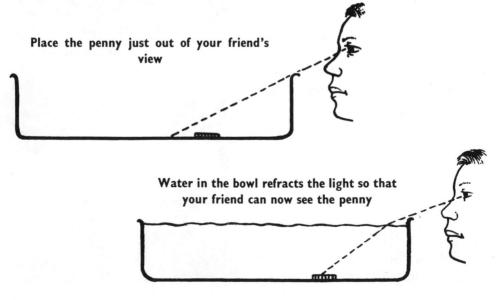

Place the penny just out of your friend's view

Water in the bowl refracts the light so that your friend can now see the penny

Make a 3-D Viewer

You will need: Card, pencil, ruler, scissors or razor blade.

Without expense, you can make a stereoscopic viewer which will let your eyes play tricks with your vision.

With the aid of pencil and ruler draw a simple cross in the middle of a piece of thin cardboard. The legs of the cross should be about 2 inches long by half an inch wide. Cut the cross away, leaving the card intact.

When the cross has been removed, place the card at right-angles in a vertical position in front of a picture or photograph.

Look down through the cross at the picture (photographs of buildings give good results) and after a few seconds the picture will appear to stand out in three dimensions. It helps if you *expect* to see a three-dimensional view, as we so often see just what we expect.

Photographs of buildings work particularly well

The Whistle and the Funnel

You will need: A whistle, funnel, string.

Insert the end of a round whistle into the stem of a funnel so that they fit firmly together. Tie one end of a length of string to the funnel and the other end to the whistle.

Swing the funnel and the whistle will blow

Whirl this equipment in a circle and the whistle will blow a note. The air which is forced through the funnel into the whistle causes it to blow.

Now let a friend swing the funnel horizontally while you stand to one side so that the whistle first approaches and then retreats from you on its circular course.

In your position, the note from the whistle will seem to rise and fall like a siren. (This is called "Doppler's effect.") Your friend, however, will hear only one tone.

The siren you hear is known as Doppler's effect

You

Friend

A Simple Thermometer

You will need: Glass tube, cork, bottle, bowl, water, kettle.

Thermometers depend for their action upon the fact that fluids expand when heated and contract when cooled. Most thermometers use mercury to register degrees of heat. We will make a simple form of thermometer using water.

Pour a cupful of water into a bottle and stand the bottle in a bowl. Drill a hole in the cork and insert a length of glass tube that reaches well below the surface of the water when you cork the bottle tightly.

Now heat some water in a kettle and pour it over the bottle. This will heat the water in the bottle and cause it to rise in the tube.

Now pour cold water over the outside of the bottle and the water will gradually sink lower in your home-made thermometer.

As the water expands it rises up in the glass tube

Compressing Air under Water

You will need: Rubber tube, jar, bowl of water.

When Scuba divers descend into the depths of the ocean they carry their own air with them so that they can breathe below the surface. The tank isn't large, because it is possible to press a large amount of air into a comparatively small container.

You can make your own container of compressed air under water.

Place a jar in a bowl of water and allow it to fill before standing it upside down with the end of a rubber tube trapped inside it.

Blow into the tube and you will see the water level fall inside the jar as you force air into it. Release the end of the tube and you will hear the hiss of escaping air. You will also notice the water rise again in the jar.

It takes a lot of air to move a little water because the air is compressed in the closed space.

How a Filter Works

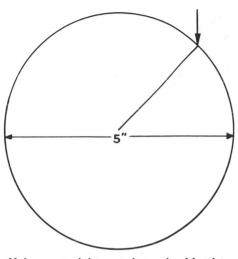

You will need: Blotting paper, paper clip, water and glass, sand, salt, sugar, ink.

When you turn on the faucet and fill a glass with water you must have noticed how clean and sparkling the water looks. This is because it has been filtered and chemically treated to remove impurities, for impure drinking water can cause illness.

When you stir sand into water it never dissolves, but remains suspended in the water. A filter can be used to remove suspended substances from liquids, but it cannot

Make a straight cut into the blotting paper

remove dissolved matter, such as salt.

You can make a simple filter by cutting a circle of blotting paper about 5 inches in diameter, and making a straight cut into this circle from the outside to the center, as shown in the diagram.

Form several shallow cones from the blotting paper, securing the ends with a paper clip. Place a cone in the top of a glass.

Now try the effect of your filter on a sand-water mixture; on a salt mixture; on a sugar mixture; on an ink-and-water mixture, etc. You must use a fresh filter cone each time, of course. It will be easy for you to discover which are the suspended substances and which have been fully dissolved.

The Obedient Can

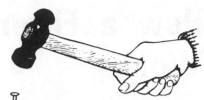

You will need: A round can with lid, nail, hammer, rubber bands, thread, nut and bolt.

Your knowledge of the force of gravity will enable you to construct a simple mechanical toy which will obediently return when you roll it away.

Make two holes in the lid and two holes in the bottom of the can

Weight tied to rubber band where it crosses in the center of the can

Begin by hammering two holes in the lid and two holes in the bottom of the can with a nail.

Cut a long rubber band (or several knotted together) and pass it through the four holes in figure-of-eight fashion. See diagram. Tie ends of the rubber band together again.

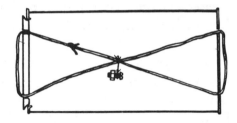

Now tie a small weight, such as a piece of lead or nut and bolt, to the center of the rubber band, where it crosses inside the can.

Replace the lid and roll the can away from you. The weight supplies a lowered center of gravity which winds up the rubber band. When the force you have used has been expended, the band will unwind and the can will slowly roll back to you.

The thicker the rubber band, the quicker the toy will return.

Expansion Race

You will need: Three small bottles of similar size, three glass tubes, water, turpentine, rubbing alcohol, bowl.

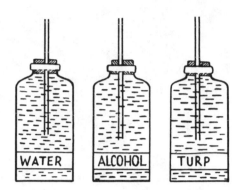
Fill the bottles with three different fluids

Obtain three small bottles of the same size, each with a well-fitting cork. Drill holes in the corks to receive lengths of glass tubing.

Fill the bottles with different liquids, e.g., water, turpentine, rubbing alcohol, etc. Label each bottle and keep them away from flames.

Pour hot (but not boiling) water into a bowl and stand the three jars in the water. As the liquids become heated they will expand—but not to an equal degree.

The only escape for the expanding liquids is via the glass tubes. You will soon see which liquid wins this race of expansion. The alcohol will reach a higher point in its tube than the turpentine, thus indicating that it has a higher rate of expansion at the same temperature. The water will be found the least expansive of the three fluids.

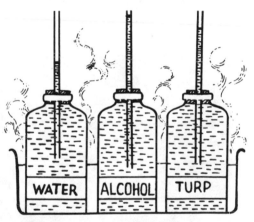
The alcohol reaches a higher point than the other liquids

Try this same experiment with other fluids.

Test by Fire

Make a note of the chemical you hold in the flame and any color it produces

A crystal of copper sulfate will supply a fine, blue flame

You will need: Candle, salt, copper sulfate, boric acid, tongs.

When scientists are asked to find out what certain substances are composed of, they are said to analyze these materials.

One of the instruments they may use is a spectroscope. This instrument records the colors of the flame a substance produces when it burns, for each element produces a definite color of its own.

You can prove this by holding various chemicals over a candle flame with tongs.

Common household salt should give off a yellow flame from the sodium which is present. Boric acid will give a greenish flame from the boron which is present.

If you can obtain a crystal of copper sulfate from a druggist you will find that it will produce a beautiful blue flame.

A Liquid Sandwich

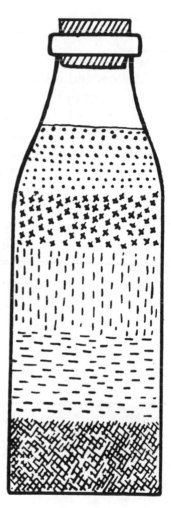

You will need: Water, ink, salad oil, glycerin, small bottle with cork.

Pour a little oil and an equal amount of water into a small bottle. Cork the bottle well and then shake it vigorously. The water and oil will appear to mix, but when you set the bottle down you will see them separate from each other. Soon the oil will be floating on top of the water. No matter how hard you shake the bottle you will never be able to make the two combine.

Sailors sometimes pour heavy oil on the sea to calm the surface for rescue work.

Try the effect of mixing other fluids. Use ink to distinguish between them if they are of similar color. With care and experiment, it is possible to fill a bottle with layers of different colored fluids, allowing heavy liquids, such as glycerin, to have first entry into the bottle.

Mirror Writing

You will need: Small mirror, pen or pencil, paper.

Mirrors and other smooth, polished surfaces reflect light. We see reflections from such surfaces because the rays of light form an image on the retina of our eyes.

Such images are always reversed. Look at yourself in a mirror, wink your right eye and your left eye seems to wink back at you.

Wink your right eye and watch your left eye wink back

You can use a mirror to send a coded message to a friend. Stand a mirror upright on the table, so that a piece of paper on the table can be clearly seen in the mirror.

Now write a message that looks right when you look in the mirror. Keep your eyes on the reflected image while you are writing and not on your paper. After a little practice you will find it easy to write "backwards."

When your friend receives such a message he will be able to read it by holding the paper up to a mirror.

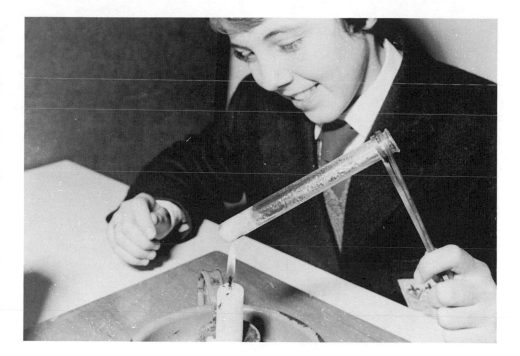

Invisible Water

You will need: Soda, test tube, tongs, candle.

Water is present in varying degrees in many apparently solid substances. Our own bodies consist of a very high percentage of water. Even such substances as ordinary washing soda (or sodium carbonate, to give it its correct chemical name) contains a large proportion of water. This can be verified by a simple experiment.

Take a spoonful of soda and drop it into the bottom of a test tube.

Hold the tube by the tongs and allow a candle flame to play on the end of the test tube containing the soda. Within a short time, the soda will become damp and you will see water vapor rise up inside the test tube, and condense on the cooler sides of the tube. This water had originally been part of the soda crystals.

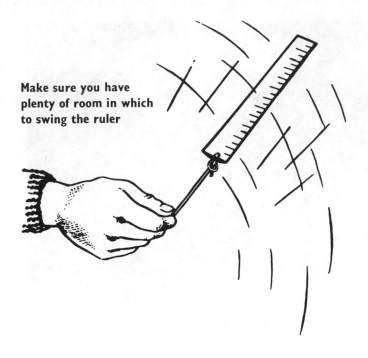

Make sure you have plenty of room in which to swing the ruler

The Roaring Ruler

You will need: A ruler, string, drill or gimlet.

Find an old ruler and bore a small hole near one end, being careful not to split the wood.

Take about 2 feet of thin, strong twine and tie one end to the hole in the ruler.

You will need a clear space for this experiment so we suggest you try it outdoors. Whirl the ruler around as fast as you can. The ruler will emit a roar that is quite startling. The sound is caused by vibrations of the twine.

Try the same experiment with differently shaped pieces of plywood and see what difference in sound you can achieve. Try attaching the ruler to a loop of twine and see what happens when there are two strings to vibrate as you whirl the ruler.

Capillary Filtering

You will need: Two bowls, water, knitting wool or flannel strips, earth.

Here is another way of filtering suspended matter from water. This time, instead of blotting paper we will use a wick which you can make from a thin strip of flannel or several strands of knitting wool woven to form a thin "rope."

Stir some earth into a bowl of water. The earth will not dissolve, but will remain suspended and will discolor the water.

Now comes the problem of filtering the water so that it will once again be clean and free from earth.

Raise the bowl of muddy water onto a box or pile of books and suspend a length of wick over one side so that it hangs down into a lower bowl.

After a time you will notice that drops of clear water are falling from the free end of the wick. Capillary attraction draws the water from the top bowl down into the lower bowl, but the suspended matter is left behind.

The same arrangement can be made to ensure that a favorite plant receives regular watering while you are away on a vacation. Place a bowl of water on a box, above the plant. Connect the water to the earth in the plant pot by means of a single thread of wool. While you are absent, water will flow slowly along the wool and down into the plant pot, keeping the earth nicely moistened.

Water will flow from the top bowl but the earth will be filtered out

A Miniature Diving Bell

You will need: Handkerchief, water glass, bowl of water.

Scientists have explored great depths of the sea by being lowered in diving bells. Usually air is pumped down from the surface, although some bells have compressed air cylinders.

It is possible for us to make a miniature diving bell from an ordinary upturned water glass.

First, roll a handkerchief into a ball and wedge it tightly into the bottom of the glass. Turning the glass upside down, make quite sure that the handkerchief remains in position. Then push the glass vertically into the water, and keep your hand on top of the glass so that it does not overturn.

Remove the glass from the water and retrieve your handkerchief—it is still perfectly dry! The reason for this is the fact that air trapped in the glass, as it was lowered below the surface, prevented water from entering the tumbler.

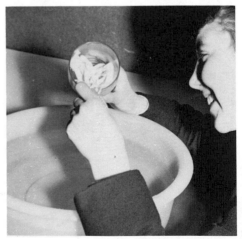

Table-Top Indian

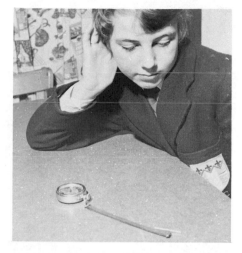

A cupped hand at the ear will help magnify sound

You will need: A watch.

Have you ever seen Western pictures where the Indian places his ear to the ground to listen for galloping horses?

We can prove that it is possible to hear galloping or any sound at a much greater distance in this way.

Sounds are carried more clearly through the earth than through the air.

Place a watch on top of the table at sufficient distance so that you can just hear it ticking. Cup your hand around your ear and notice how it helps to magnify the sound slightly.

Now place your ear on the table top. Notice how much more clearly you can hear the watch ticking? This is because the sound waves travel more easily through the wood than through the air.

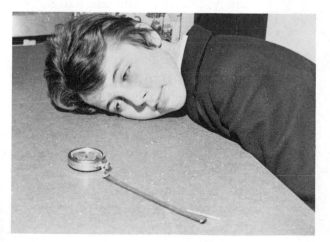

Listen Indian fashion, with your ear to the table

The Inert Coins

Problem: Remove the paper without disturbing the coins

You will need: Three coins, water glass, paper, ruler.

Have you ever seen a magician snatch a cloth from a table, leaving all the crockery and cutlery still in position? This feat is made possible by the condition known to scientists as "inertia." The cloth was whipped away so quickly that the articles on top of it were left comparatively undisturbed.

You can perform the same trick on a smaller level.

First, cut a long slip of drawing paper, place one end on the edge of a glass and balance three coins on top of it, as shown in the photo.

You can now remove the paper without touching the coins and still leave the latter balanced on the edge of the glass. If you pull the paper slowly, the force you use will not be enough to overcome the inertia of the coins.

So grip the free end of the paper and raise it until the paper is horizontal. Then take a ruler and strike sharply downward at the paper, about $1\frac{1}{2}$ inches away from the coins. So quickly is the paper whipped from under the coins that their inertia is undisturbed and they remain balanced on the edge of the glass.

More Inertia

You will need: A block of wood, strong thread.

Cut two pieces of strong thread and suspend a block of wood from the end of one piece. Tie the other length of thread to the underside of the wood, as shown.

This is another simple experiment in inertia. Pull slowly and steadily on the lower thread, gradually increasing the downward pressure until the upper thread breaks.

Set up again. But this time give the lower thread a sharp, powerful tug and the bottom length of thread will snap. It is because you tug sharply that the inertia of the wooden block prevents the force you are using from reaching the upper thread.

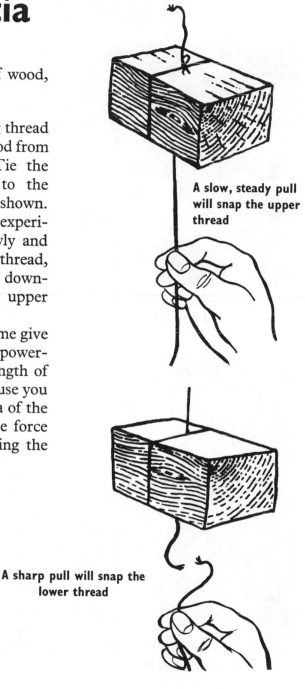

A slow, steady pull will snap the upper thread

A sharp pull will snap the lower thread

Invisible Ink

The message written in vinegar has not yet had time to dry

Warming the sheet of paper makes the invisible ink appear

You will need: A pen with a clean tip, paper, candle, vinegar or lemon juice.

Invisible ink which becomes legible when exposed to heat really employs an oxidization process. For your ink you will need either vinegar or the juice of a lemon.

Use a new tip in your pen or else thoroughly clean the old tip so that no trace of any previous ink remains. Even a sharpened matchstick can be used to write with.

Pour a little vinegar or lemon juice into an egg-cup. Write your message in large letters on a sheet of drawing paper. When the "ink" has had time to dry the message will be invisible.

To make the message reappear, hold the paper close to the flame of a candle or facing a fire, and the writing will gradually appear. This is because the portion of the paper which absorbed the vinegar or lemon juice combines with oxygen from the air more easily than the untreated area of the paper, and the writing will show up as a faint brown scorching.

Two Odd Feet

You will need: A cold floor, a mat.

When next you are standing around with bare feet, try this little experiment. Choose a floor that is quite cold—and this is true of most bathroom floors first thing in the morning!

Arrange the mat so that you can stand with one foot on the cold floor and one foot on the mat.

Which foot feels warmest? A simple question, isn't it? The reason lies in the power of some materials to conduct heat away quicker than others.

The floor allows the heat to flow rapidly

The foot on the mat remains warmer

from your foot so that it cools quickly. On the other hand (or more properly, on the other foot!) the mat is a poor conductor of heat and therefore allows that foot to retain its natural warmth.

A similar experiment can be tried with a woolen glove. Warm both hands equally, in front of a fire or on a radiator. Now put the glove on one of your hands. Because wool is a bad conductor of heat the gloved hand will retain its warmth for a much greater time than the other.

On the Smoke Trail

You will need: A candle, matches.

When we light a candle, the gas from the melting wax at the top of the candle rises to combine with the oxygen in the air and to give us a flame.

We can make the flame leap down instead of up in another way. First light the candle. Then blow it out and immediately hold a lighted match, in readiness, just above the top of the stream of smoke. This flame will leap backward down the gas in the smoke and ignite the wick again.

Watch Your Pulse Work

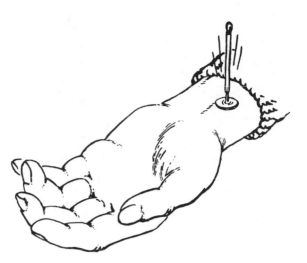

You will need: A match, thumbtack.

There are several points on your body where the blood pulsing through your arteries can be felt just under the skin.

Your blood is pumped on its surprisingly long journey (your blood vessels have a combined length of many thousands of miles) by the beating of your heart. Certain illnesses can alter the normal rhythm of this beating, which is why a doctor often feels the pulse at your wrist to see if it is regular and at a normal rate.

If you place a finger across your wrist you should have no difficulty in finding your own pulse.

Now take a thumbtack and stick the end of a wooden matchstick on the point of the pin. Position the head of the thumbtack above the place where you felt the pulse beat at your wrist. Now hold your hand and arm perfectly still and you will see a slight but regular movement of the match as it moves to the pulsing of your blood beneath the head of the thumbtack.

INDEX